Artist Quality products created by Artists

SCHOOL OF COLOUR PUBLICATIONS

by Craig Letourneau
and Michael Wilcox

ISBN 1-931780-12-9
Text, Illustrations and Arrangement Copyright:
The Michael Wilcox School of Colour Publishing Ltd.
Gibbet Lane, Whitchurch
Bristol BS14 OBX
England
Tel: UK 01275 835500
Facsimile: UK 01275 892659
First published 2002

Distributed in the UK, EEC and associated territories by:
Search Press Limited
Wellwood, North Farm Road
Tunbridge Wells, Kent
TN2 3DR, England
Tel: (01892) 510850
Facsimile: (01892) 515903
Email sales@searchpress.com
Website www.searchpress.com

Distributed to the trade and art markets in Australia by:
Keith Ainsworth Pty Ltd
Unit 6/88 Batt Street
Penrith NSW 2750
PO Box 6061
Tel: 02 47 323411
Facsimile: 02 47 218259
Email: ainsbrook@ozemail.com.au

Scanning and colour balance:
Paul Goodman
Planning:
Matthew Brown
Page design and layout:
Paul Goodman
Finishing:
Maureen Bonas
Artwork:
Craig Letourneau
Text:
Craig Letourneau
and Michael Wilcox
Coordination:
Anne Gardner
Printing:
Imago productions F.E. Singapore
Print coordination:
Emma Bell and Desmond Heng

Contents

Hansa Yellow and Cerulean Blue

A range of bright greens which vary in transparency from the semi transparent green-yellow to the opaque green-blue.

1	2	3	4	5	6	7	8	9	10
a	a	a	a	a	a	a	a	a	a
b	b	b	b	b	b	b	b	b	b
c	c	c	c	c	c	c	c	c	c
d	d	d	d	d	d	d	d	d	d
e	e	e	e	e	e	e	e	e	e

Throughout this publication we will be referring to the *Colour Mixing Swatch Book*. As mentioned on the back cover, you will need this publication in order to obtain the most from this and other titles in the 'Colour Notes' series.

In the example above, (which can be found on page 9 of the *Colour Mixing Swatch Book*), numbers and letters have been assigned to each hue for ease of identification.

The page number in the book is shown first, in this case 9. This is followed by the numbered colour from the top row and then the lettered tint (where applicable). Therefore, colour 9/1c is to be found on page 9. After finding page 9, go to the colour numbered 1 (top left), then down to C. This colour, 9/1c, has been circled above.

Please take a few moments to familiarise yourself with this system as we will be using it throughout the book.

Doorways can provide an interesting focus for a painting, being both intriguing and inviting. They draw the viewer in. In this painting the whitewashed wall serves as a 'canvas' for the architectural and garden features. While the roofline and climbing plants create a framework for the heart of the piece - the door.

I began by painting a very thin mix of Raw Sienna and Ultramarine, much reduced with Titanium White*, to the wall, (same as mix 1e). This gave it an off-white character. I was careful not to keep this too uniform in order to give an impression of texture as well as colour. The door was then painted using further mixes of the same two hues. Before working on the plants I first painted their shadows. Here I used a darker mix of Raw Sienna and Ultramarine. The painting was gradually built up from the limited palette that I had selected. Raw Sienna and Ultramarine was used extensively throughout, the other hues being brought in only to provide the pinks, greens and yellow greens. A good basis to work on as far as colour harmony is concerned is to obtain as many colours as possible from a single mixing pair. In this case the range to be found on page 19 of the *Colour Mixing Swatch book.*

* Please note: Although this was a watercolour, I used white paint, rather than employ the white of the paper, in order to obtain the colours that I wanted. A vast range of tints can *only* be produced with the use of white

Phthalocyanine Green and
Quinacridone Violet P21

2c   3a   3b   6a   2d

Raw Sienna and
Ultramarine P1

7a

3d

6

4d

9e

9d

7a

2c

4c

2c

7b

Hansa Yellow and
Phthalocyanine Green P14

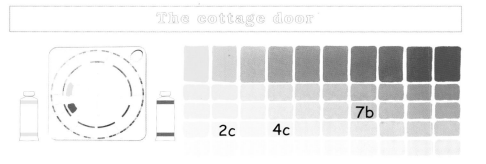

Hansa Yellow and Phthalocyanine Green P14

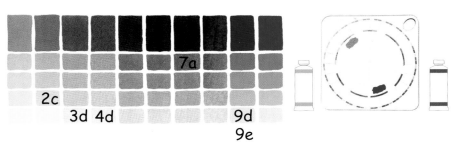

Raw Sienna and Ultramarine Blue P19

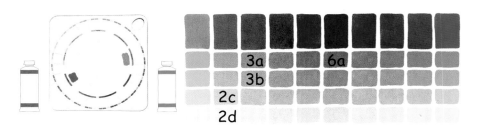

Phthalocyanine Green and Quinacridone Violet P21

This painting was a good exercise in the use of greys. For a painter, a very useful way to produce greys is to combine orange and blue, a complementary pair. These will give a wide range of 'coloured greys'. Cadmium Yellow Light and Cadmium Red Light was first mixed to give a bright orange. I then added the Cerulean Blue. Substituting Ultramarine for Cerulean Blue will give even darker 'coloured greys' with the orange. (Page 45 of the swatch book). Burnt Sienna, (which is essentially a dull orange) mixed with Ultramarine will produce *very* dark greys, approaching black. (Page 48).

8

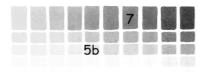

5b 7

Ultramarine and
Hansa Yellow P10

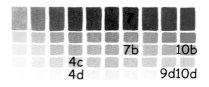

4c
4d 7b 10b
9d10d

Yellow Ochre and
Ultramarine P18

1
1a

Phthalocyanine and
Quinacridone P21

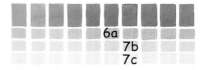

6a
7b
7c

Orange and
Cerulean P44

I began with a very light application of Yellow Ochre and
Ultramarine to all of the stonework. The mix was the same
as 4e from page 18. I was careful to avoid painting over the
white window frames and highlights of the plants and pots.
This same mixing pair were then used to establish the
darker areas and also to form the shadows.
The 'coloured greys' from a mixed orange and Cerulean Blue
were used for the forecourt. The plants were painted using
Ultramarine Blue and Hansa Yellow, a mixing pair which give
a useful range of mid-intensity greens. Quinacridone Violet
was used for the flowers.

Yellow Ochre and
Ultramarine P18

10b 10d 4c 4d 9d 7b 7

Ultramarine and
Hansa Yellow P10

7 5b

7b 7c 6a
Orange and
Cerulean P44

1a 1
Phthalocyanine
Green and
Quinacridone
Violet P21

As with all of the paintings, only the more important mixes have been identified. To show all of the combinations would be impossible. If producing these paintings yourself, you will find the other mixes on the relevant colour mixing swatch. Many are simply lighter or darker versions of the identified colours.

 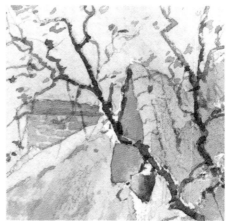

I began this painting with Cerulean and Phthalocyanine Blue to the sky. This was followed by a pale wash of Quinacridone Violet and Ultramarine Blue to the face of the cottage. A little Titanium white was added to this mixture to dull the pink. White will always dull and 'cool' a colour. It is important to know that a vast range of tints cannot be produced without the occasional use of white; 'Chalky' pinks amongst them.

When fully dry I painted my shadows under the roof lines using Cerulean Blue and Burnt Sienna. This gave much needed definition to the pale painting. I then added the greenery, making sure to vary the values to add interest. Cerulean Blue and Burnt Sienna, a very useful mixing pair, were used to paint the rest of the building. The flowers were added at the end.

Cerulean Blue and Burnt Sienna P46

9b 9c 3d 3 6e 4c 6c 4a

Cerulean and
Phthalocyanine
Blue P50
4d

5c

3e

2d

1a

5c

4b

9b
Quinacridone and
Ultramarine P22

6a 6b 4
Hansa Yellow and Cerulean Blue P9

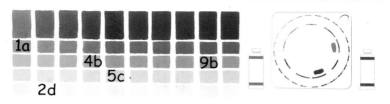

1a
4b
5c
2d
9b

Quinacridone Violet and Ultramarine Blue P22

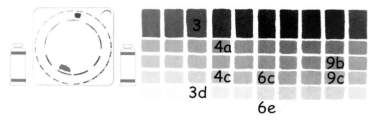

3
4a
4c
3d
6c
6e
9b
9c

Cerulean Blue and Burnt Sienna P46

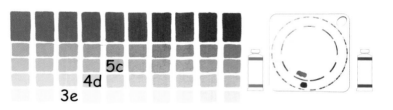

5c
4d
3e

Cerulean Blue and Phthalocyanine Blue P50

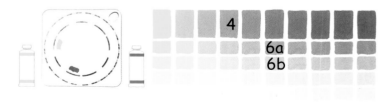

4
6a
6b

Hansa Yellow and Cerulean Blue P9

15

Sometimes a cottage painting relies on a feature such as a door or window to give focus. In this simple study I painted the walls a very pale Cerulean Blue and Burnt Sienna mix. Whilst this was still wet, Quinacridone and Ultramarine blends were used for the shadows. All the green foliage and flowers were painted loosely and expressively using the mixtures shown. Only a few of these mixes are identified, others you will find on the relevant mixing swatch. The whites of the painted window frames were painted with Cerulean and Burnt Sienna, lightened and dulled to a great extent with Titanium White, the colour was similar to 3e page 46 and was applied very thinly to avoid 'chalkiness. The presence of Titanium White for painted woodwork helps, in my opinion, to give a 'realistic' feel.

Cerulean Blue and
Burnt Sienna P46
3e 5e 5c

Quinacridone and
Ultramarine P22
9c 3b 8 9a

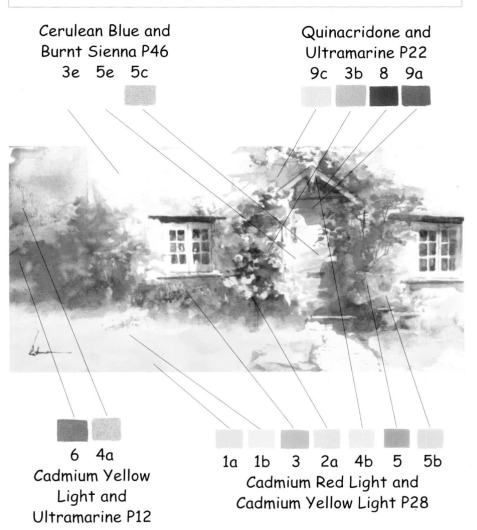

6 4a
Cadmium Yellow
Light and
Ultramarine P12

1a 1b 3 2a 4b 5 5b
Cadmium Red Light and
Cadmium Yellow Light P28

The locations of these mixes are shown on the following page. You will learn a great deal about colour mixing by studying the mixing swatches.

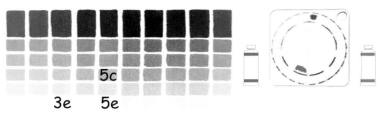

5c

3e   5e

Cerulean Blue and Burnt Sienna P46

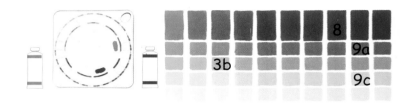

Quinacridone Violet and Ultramarine Blue P22

Cadmium Yellow Light and Ultramarine Blue P12

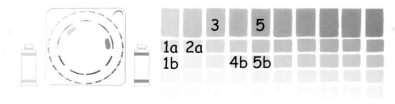

Cadmium Yellow Light and Cadmium Red Light P28

In this painting I wanted too illustrate a row of cottages of various textures, in both sunlight and shadow.
Careful attention was given to making sure a wide range of values (light to dark), were present. If you notice the light striking the roof of the centre cottage it clearly shows the difference in value between shaded areas and those in direct sunlight. One way to think of value difference is to imagine a scene as a black and white photograph. There would be a clear difference in value between the well lit and the shaded area of the roof in question in such a photograph. I used a mixed bright orange (from Cadmium Red Light and Cadmium Yellow Light) plus Cerulean Blue for the faces of most of the cottages. You can obtain 'warm' 'coloured greys' from this range, (as depicted in the cottage on the far left). Blends of these two hues will also give a good range of 'brick' colours.

Cerulean and
Ultramarine P49
5d

Raw Sienna and
Ultramarine P19
8a   8   4b   6   9a   8   4

8e   4d   8d   3b   3a   7a   5e
Bright Orange and
Cerulean P44

2a   2c   7   7a
Cad Yellow and
Ultramarine P12

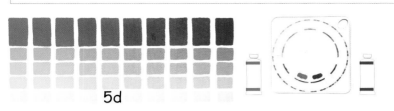

5d

Cerulean Blue and Ultramarine Blue P49

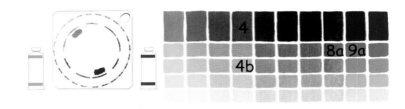

4
8a 9a
4b

Raw Sienna and Ultramarine Blue P19

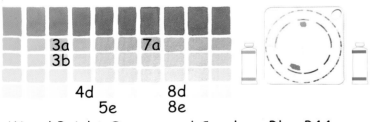

3a   7a
3b
4d   8d
5e   8e

Mixed Bright Orange and Cerulean Blue P44

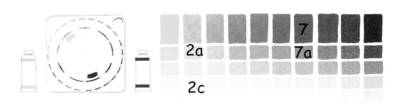

2a
7
7a
2c

Cad Yellow and Ultramarine Blue P12

This painting relies heavily on the complimentary orange-blue relationship. I began with a simple wash of Cerulean Blue and Ultramarine to the sky. I also used this combination for the water, the shadowed side of the cottage, in the boat and on the steps. The range from any of the mixing swatches can be made to harmonise quite readily. In this case the different blues are easy to work together. By repeating a basic colour in different parts of a painting, visual interest can be added. The dull oranges have also been dispersed around the painting for the same reason.

Cerulean Blue and
Ultramarine P49
7d   7b   7c

Quinacridone and
Ultramarine P22
3c   3b   3a

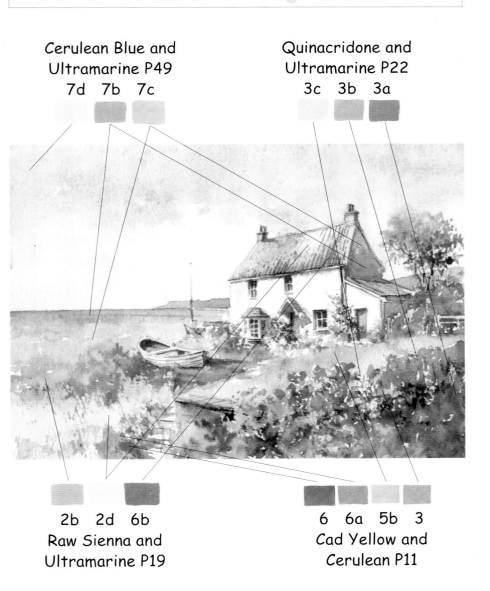

2b   2d   6b
Raw Sienna and
Ultramarine P19

6   6a   5b   3
Cad Yellow and
Cerulean P11

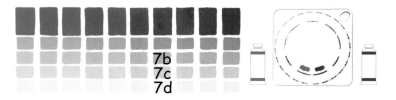

Cerulean Blue and Ultramarine Blue P49

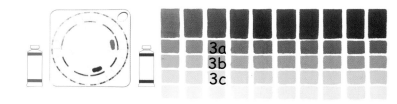

Quinacridone Violet and Ultramarine Blue P22

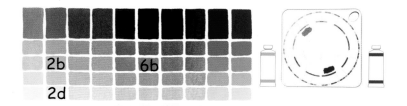

Raw Sienna and Ultramarine Blue P19

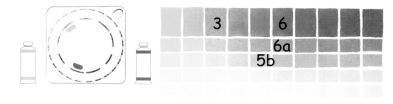

Cad Yellow and Cerulean Blue P11

The complementary pairs, blue/orange, yellow/violet and red/green can add visual interest to a painting. In this piece I used the blue/orange combination as the main complementary pair, followed by an interplay of yellow and violet in the bottom right corner.

This simple study began with a wash of Cerulean Blue and Ultramarine to areas of the sky. Whilst this was still wet, various blends of Hansa Yellow and Raw Sienna was added to the unpainted areas of the sky and allowed to blend into the blue here and there. Mixes from the same combination were brushed over all the ground right up to the horizon. Whilst the painting was still damp, Raw Sienna and Ultramarine blends were applied to form the background trees. I was careful when working wet into wet to avoid painting over the shape that would be the cottage. As the paper began to dry I added the plants in the foreground. After the paper was totally dry I painted the cottage using a range of mixes from orange and Cerulean Blue.

Cerulean and
Ultramarine P49
4d   9d

Hansa and
Raw Sienna P53
5c   3d   3c   6c   6a

1b   3a   7a   6   8
Mixed Bright Orange
and Cerulean P44

6a   8   6
Raw Sienna and
Ultramarine P19

The left side of the roof was painted a bright orange to
compliment the blues in the background. The mixes from the
individual swatches are identified on the following page.

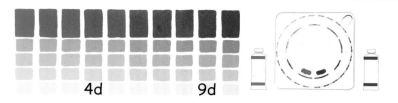

Cerulean Blue and Ultramarine Blue P49

Hansa Yellow and Raw Sienna P53

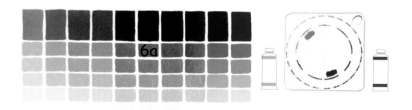

Raw Sienna and Ultramarine Blue P19

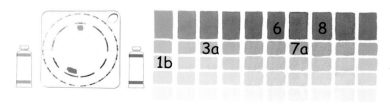

Mixed Bright Orange and Cerulean Blue P44

With careful use, a complementary pair can add visual interest and bring colour harmony to a painting. The Impressionists made great use of complementaries, particularly blue and orange. Although many approaches can be taken, one very effective technique is to apply the chosen pair very lightly, side by side. As you will see from the front wall of this cottage, the effect can add life and interest to what could otherwise be a rather dull section of a painting. The blue/orange combination is used in a more direct way between the roof and the sky.

Cerulean and
Burnt Sienna P46

5a	5c	3b	5	3d	5a

Raw Sienna and
Ultramarine P19

5	3d	2d	2c

8c	2e	8a	8e

Mixed Orange and
Cerulean P44

Cerulean Blue and Burnt Sienna P46

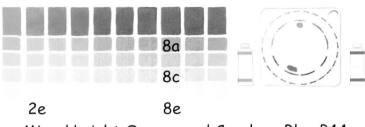

Mixed bright Orange and Cerulean Blue P44

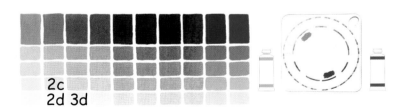

Raw Sienna and Ultramarine Blue P19

It will pay to spend a moment familiarising yourself with the mixes and where they can be found on the colour swatches.

In this street scene I used mixes of Quinacridone Violet and Ultramarine to provide the shading on the buildings. Notice how the shadows get slightly lighter as they travel down the buildings. Also that the well lit areas appear much brighter and lighter when placed next to the shadows. I began the painting with Cerulean Blue dulled very slightly with orange for the sky. This particularly useful combination will give a wide range of colours and 'temperatures'. The blue will neutralise, or dull, the orange and vice versa. Around the middle of the range a series of 'coloured greys' will emerge. Such greys can be balanced against the rest of the hues in the range to bring colour harmony to a painting.

Mixed Bright Orange
and Cerulean Blue P44

1   3c   7   5d   9d   6c   9e   5a   2d   2c   2e   9b

2b   1e   7a
Hansa Yellow and
Ultramarine P10

1b   9b   6d   8c
uinacridone Violet and
Ultramarine P22

7a   7c
Raw Sienna and
Ultramarine P19

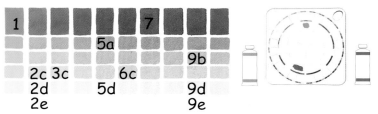

Mixed Bright Orange and Cerulean Blue P46

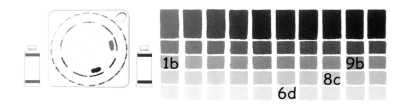

Quinacridone Violet and Ultramarine Blue P22

Hansa Yellow and Ultramarine Blue P10

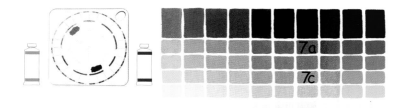

Raw Sienna and Ultramarine Blue P19

A very good exercise in colour mixing would be to make simple drawings of the above studies. Then mix and apply the colours that were used in the original. To add to the value of this exercise, try using completely different mixtures taken from other pages of the *Colour Mixing Swatch book.*

I began this painting with a wash of Cerulean Blue and Ultramarine to the sky. Intermixing the various blues will give a very extensive range of possible sky colours. Such mixes can be found on pages 49, 50 and 51 of the *Color Mixing Swatch book*. Further blues can be obtained by modifying either Phthalocyanine Blue, Cerulean Blue or Ultramarine. Examples of such modification will be found throughout the swatch book. I choose not to use Cobalt Blue, although it can be an excellent colour. I find that I can mix similar blues with ease and many manufactured 'Cobalt Blues' are simple mixes anyway, rather than the genuine pigment. For the various greens in the painting I used blends of Hansa Yellow and Phthalocyanine Blue. Such mixes are very bright and very clear. They are bright because both hues bring a lot of green into the mix and they are clear because the blue is extremely transparent and the yellow is semi-transparent.

Cadmium Red Light
and Ultramarine P23
3a   3c

Raw Sienna and
Ultramarine P19
7a   6b   3c   7   7a

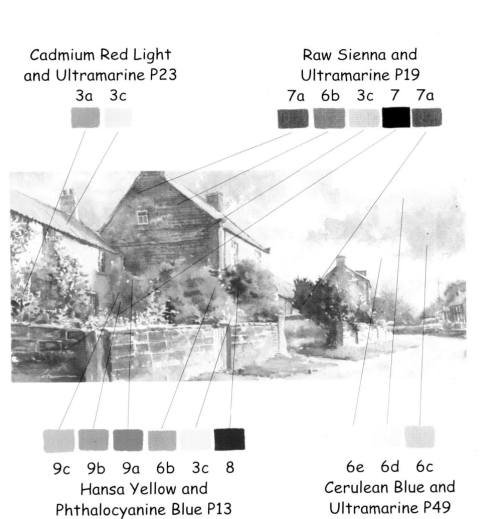

9c   9b   9a   6b   3c   8
Hansa Yellow and
Phthalocyanine Blue P13

6e   6d   6c
Cerulean Blue and
Ultramarine P49

Hansa Yellow and
Phthalocyanine Blue P13

Raw Sienna and Ultramarine
P19

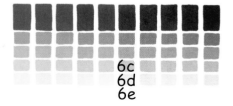

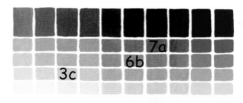

Cerulean and Ultramarine
P49

Cad Red and Ultramarine P23

We have looked very briefly at the use of complementary pairings, with examples of blue/orange and violet/red. The third major pair is red and green. In this painting I wanted to draw the eye of the viewer to the cottage roof. By using a backdrop of green to the orange-red roof I was able to add the red/green combination to the blue/orange complementaries used elsewhere in the work. When a colour such as red is placed alongside green, or surrounded by green, our visual system can actually enhance the red, making it appear brighter. Used with care such combinations can add either harmony or a very subtle contrast to a painting.

Cerulean and
Ultramarine P49
9b 9d

Cadmium Red Light and
Bright Green P32
1d 1a 9b

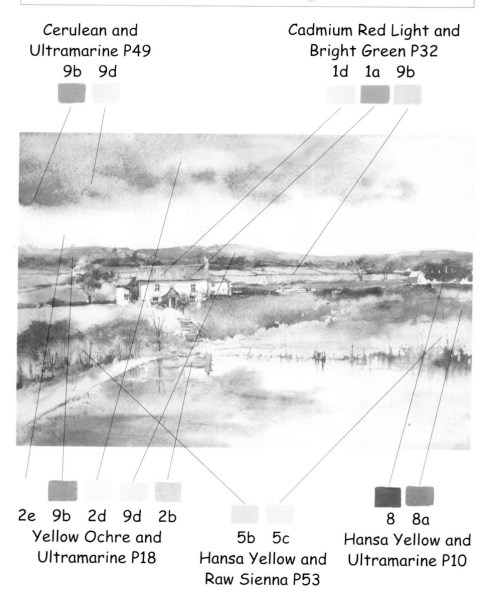

2e 9b 2d 9d 2b
Yellow Ochre and
Ultramarine P18

5b 5c
Hansa Yellow and
Raw Sienna P53

8 8a
Hansa Yellow and
Ultramarine P10

Hansa Yellow and
Ultramarine Blue P10

Yellow Ochre and
Ultramarine Blue P18

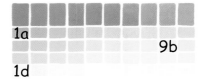

Cad Red and
Bright Green P32

Cerulean Blue and
Ultramarine Blue P49

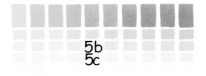

Hansa Yellow and
Raw Sienna P53

By placing various greens around the orange-red roof I was
able to take advantage of the special relationship between
these two basic hues. Red and green are a valuable
complementary pair with many applications.

41

This stone cottage relies largely on value contrast to stand out in the landscape. I deliberately surrounded the light coloured roofs with darker colour to draw attention to them through the contrast of light and dark.

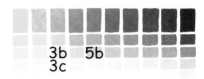

3b 5b
3c

Cadmium Yellow Light and Ultramarine Blue P12

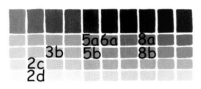

5a6a 8a
3b 5b 8b
2c
2d

Raw Sienna and Ultramarine Blue P19

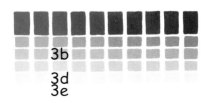

3b
3d
3e

Cerulean Blue and Ultramarine Blue P49

As you will see throughout the book, many of the colours used are simply lighter or darker versions of other hues in use. In the example to the left, once the initial mix had been made (3b) I simply used lighter versions of it.

Cerulean and
Ultramarine P49
3e   3d   3b

Raw Sienna and
Ultramarine P19

8a

2c

8b

5b

5a

2d

3b

6a

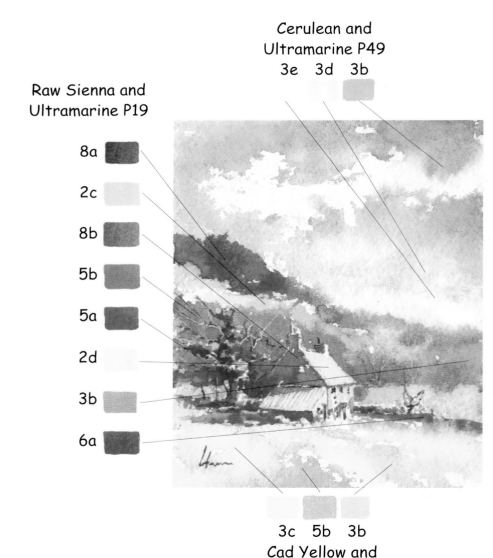

3c   5b   3b
Cad Yellow and
Ultramarine P12

I found this attractive country pub particularly appealing, with its interesting architectural features as well as its liquid offerings.
I started by loosely painting in a varied ultramarine wash to the sky. Whilst the paper was still damp, I added the background trees. I applied masking fluid to what would be the foliage highlights and lines in the brickwork. This gave me the ability to paint expressively knowing I could later reclaim these valuable highlights. A very pale mixed orange was used to paint the face of the building.
I used Titanium White to lighten the mix in order to give the colour a 'chalky' feel.

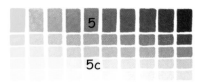

Cadmium Yellow Light
and Ultramarine Blue P12

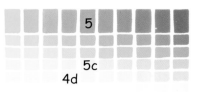

Cadmium Yellow Light
and Cadmium Red Light
P26

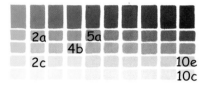

Mixed Bright Orange
and Ultramarine P45

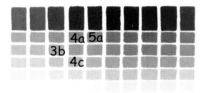

Cerulean Blue and
Ultramarine P46

Watercolourists who avoid the use of white do so at the expense of a vast range of tints. Many colours simply cannot be produced without the use of white. Its use will dull and 'cool' a colour and make otherwise transparent hues more opaque. These very factors give us tints which would otherwise be unavailable. Many a watercolour purist would shun white but quite happily use such colours as Naples Yellow in their work. Modern Naples Yellow is basically a mix of Cadmium Yellow and White. It is a colour which simply cannot be produced any other way.

Mixed Bright Orange
and Ultramarine P45
5a 2c 2a 4b 10c 10e

5c   5   4d
Cad Yellow and
Cad Red P26

5   5c
Cad Yellow and
Ultramarine P12

4a 4c 3b 5a 4a
Cerulean Blue and
Burnt Sienna P46

47

This simple winter cottage study began with a wash of Cerulean Blue and Ultramarine to the sky. I was careful to allow changes in value (light/dark) to add interest. Then pale Raw Sienna and Ultramarine mixes were washed over the snow, becoming darker where shadows were introduced.

The background trees were then laid in and blended into the still damp sky. When dry, the cottage was painted with various mixes of Raw Sienna and Ultramarine. The same Cerulean Blue and Ultramarine combination as used in the sky was employed to paint the snow covered roofs.

Cerulean and
Ultramarine P49
7d   9e   9c   7b

Hansa and
Ultramarine P10
8a   8

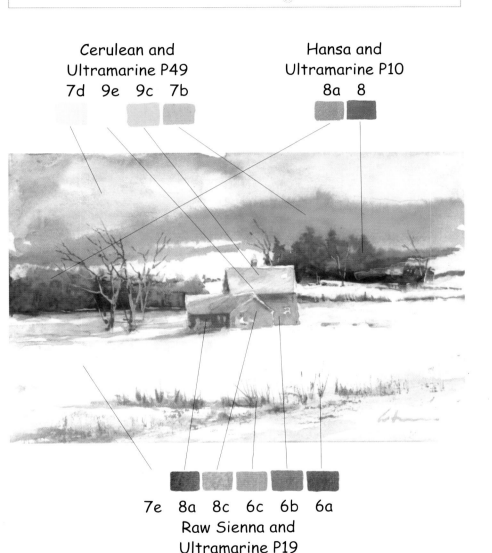

7e   8a   8c   6c   6b   6a
Raw Sienna and
Ultramarine P19

There is a certain mystery to an isolated cottage within a broad landscape. A single building, framed by open country, has inspired artists for centuries.

In this painting I wanted the background, sky and foreground to be unified in terms of colour. Therefore I used mixes available from the Hansa Yellow/Raw Sienna range in these areas. This approach can help to hold a painting together.

I began the piece with washes from this swatch to the sky. Once I was happy with the sky I moved down to the background and then painted in the foreground. I made sure that the sky was slightly darker than the ground. Whilst wet, I added touches of a Raw Sienna and Ultramarine mix into the sky.

Burnt Sienna and
Ultramarine P48
5a 5b 7a 7d 4c

Raw Sienna
and Ultramarine P19
8a

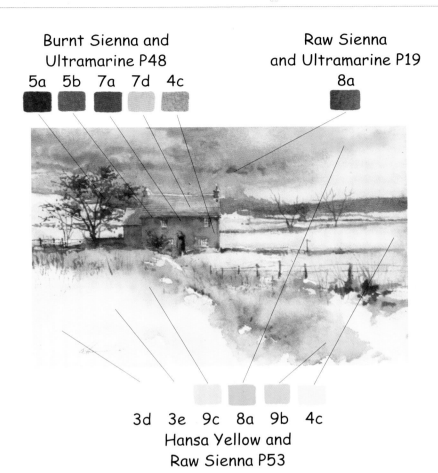

3d 3e 9c 8a 9b 4c
Hansa Yellow and
Raw Sienna P53

When the paper was bone dry, I painted the cottage using
Burnt Sienna and Ultramarine, gradually making it darker
towards the left, more shadowed side of the structure. As a
final touch I added the front door using Cadmium Red Light.

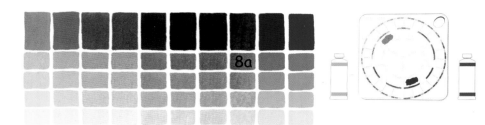

Raw Sienna and Ultramarine Blue Page 19 of the
Colour Mixing Swatch Book

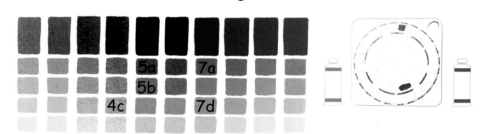

Burnt Sienna and Ultramarine Blue Page 48 of the
Colour Mixing Swatch Book

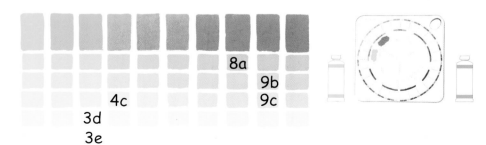

Hansa Yellow and Raw Sienna Page 53 of the
Colour Mixing Swatch Book

By repeating the use of dulled orange yellows throughout
the painting, a certain unity was achieved. Being high in value
(light), this colour range allowed a strong contrast when
darker hues were set against it. Such light/dark contrasts
can be invaluable as far as adding visual interest
is concerned.

I have always enjoyed painting white coastal cottages. Upon close observation we can see that the white is actually not white but a very pale 'coloured grey'. The water itself was actually a lighter value than the white of the cottage. Only two colour combinations were used to paint this quick study. I began with mixed bright orange and Cerulean Blue for the sky and sea, varying the values throughout. When dry, Burnt Sienna and Ultramarine blends were used for the foreground and cottage.

54

Mixed Bright Orange
and Cerulean P44
8a   8d   8c   1e   1c   1d

4e   4   4a   8c
Burnt Sienna and
Ultramarine P48

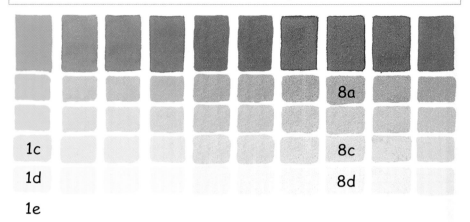

Bright Mixed Orange and Cerulean Blue Page 44 of the Colour Mixing Swatch Book.

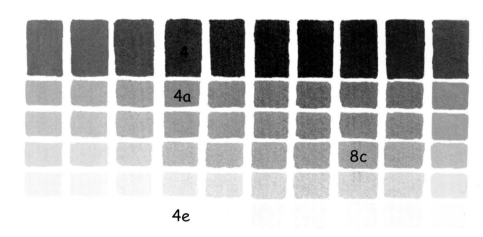

Burnt Sienna and Cerulean Blue Page 46 of the Colour Mixing Swatch Book.

It would be too time consuming and distracting for an artist to paint every brick in a cottage. Not only this, but the final result could well look more like a technical drawing than a painting. We must therefore imply the construction through colour and texture. I used the very versatile mixed orange and Cerulean Blue combination for the brickwork exposed to direct sun light. I also used it on the sunlit roofs. Ultramarine was substituted for the Cerulean and was mixed with the same bright orange to create the shaded sides of the cottage. Simply by changing blues, I was able to use the darker blends which resulted. I was careful to leave the light window frames, fences and foliage highlights so that they could be painted later.

Mixed Bright Orange
and Ultramarine P45
5b   8   7   4a

Mixed Bright Orange
and Cerulean P44
6   3a   1c   1d

5a   5   2c   4b   7a
Cadmium Yellow
and Ultramarine P12

Cadmium Yellow Light and Ultramarine were used for
virtually all the greens. This combination will give a range of
neutralised, or dulled greens.

58

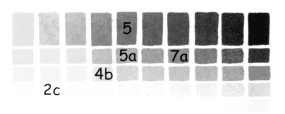

Cad Yellow and Ultramarine Page 12 of the
Colour Mixing Swatch Book.

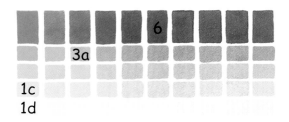

Mixed Bright Orange and Cerulean Blue Page 44 of the
Colour Mixing Swatch Book.

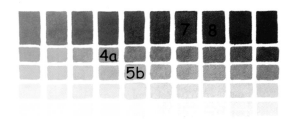

Mixed Bright Orange and Ultramarine Blue Page 45 of the
Colour Mixing Swatch Book.

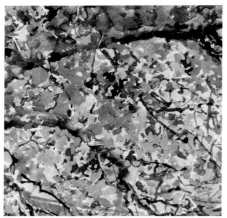

Added interest can be given to a painting by various contrasts. One of the most important being the contrast of light and dark. As you will see in the above close ups, where area of light and dark meet in a very definite way, additional visual interest is created.

In this simple grey Yorkshire stone cottage I used very few colours as an aid towards colour harmony. Various blends of Cerulean Blue and Burnt Sienna gave the hues for the sky, background and foreground. Working very loosely, I allowed them to blend in freely. I was careful to leave areas of white for the window frames and flowers so that contrasts could be maintained. A mixed yellow green neutralised, or dulled with Quinacridone Violet gave the particular greens that I needed. In order to increase the wide range of greens available from various yellow/blue combinations, try adding a little red to a green in order to reduce its intensity. This is a very efficient way to increase your range of greens. At the other end of the mixing swatch (please see next page), you will find that the green will, in turn, reduce the intensity of the red.

Mixed Yellow Green and
Quinacridone Violet P36
4 5c 2 9d 9b 2a

2d 4a 3 2b 5a 5c 5d 6b 2a 6d 4

Cerulean Blue and
Burnt Sienna P46

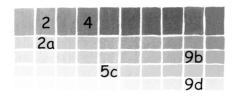

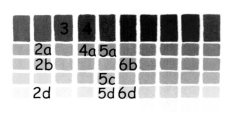

Mixed Yellow Green and
Quinacridone P36

Cerulean Blue and
Burnt Sienna P46

Cottages display a rich assortment of textured surfaces derived from the wide range of materials used in their construction. Sunlight and shade further enhance the surfaces and give added contrast. Careful observation, plus control of colour mixing, will enable you to depict these varying surfaces with whatever degree of accuracy suites your work.

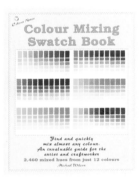

SCHOOL OF COLOUR PUBLICATIONS

A range of products has been designed and books and courses published to help bring about a fuller understanding of colour and technique. We offer paints, mixing palettes, books, courses, videos and workbooks.

For further information please contact any of the offices listed below:

The Michael Wilcox School of Color USA	The Michael Wilcox School of Colour UK	The Michael Wilcox School of Color Australia
25 Mauchly #328	Gibbet Lane	PO Box 516
Irvine	Whitchurch, Bristol	Wanneroo 6946
CA 92618 USA	BS14 0BX	Western Australia
Tel: 949 450 0266	United Kingdom	Tel: (61) 8 9405 6773
Fax: 949 450 0268	Tel: 01275 835500	Fax: (61) 8 9306 9887
Free Phone: 1888 7 WILCOX	Fax: 01275 892659	e-mail: wilcoxsoc@iinet.net.au
e-mail: wilcoxschool@earthlink.net	e-mail: wilcoxsoc@aol.com	

www.schoolofcolour.com